Of Gone Fox

Mark Goodwin & Louis Goodwin

with photos by Nikki Clayton

First published 2023 by The Hedgehog Poetry Press

Published in the UK by
The Hedgehog Poetry Press
Coppack House, 5
Churchill Avenue
Clevedon
BS21 6QW

www.hedgehogpress.co.uk

ISBN: 978-1-913499-05-1

Copyright © Mark Goodwin, Louis Goodwin & Nikki Clayton 2023

The right of Mark Goodwin, Louis Goodwin & Nikki Clayton to be identified as the authors of this work has been asserted in accordance with the Copyright, Designs and Patents Act 1988.

All rights reserved. No part of this publication may be reproduced, stored in or introduced into a retrieval system, or transmitted in any form, or by any means (electronic, mechanical, photocopying, recording or otherwise) without prior written permissions of the publisher. Any person who does any unauthorised act in relation to this publication may be liable for criminal prosecution and civil claims for damages,

9 8 7 6 5 4 3 2 1

A CIP Catalogue record for this book is available from the British Library.

for the fox pissing

Contents

Fox Caller
a fox trotting across open ground
Tess & Fox
i saw a
For Zen Fox
a fox

        Un Encounter

a fox in a fox
is fox night
Fox Go ings
Across the Ground
a fox seeing forever's fog
smart-fur red

FOX CALLER

For Russ

my brother blows his fox-lure

as sun slips away we crouch
in long grasses again

my brother blows his
rabbit-mimic a

high-pitched thin smear
of rabbity anguish vibrates

dusk's air and

again my brother blows so
         it seems a rabbit's voice

repeatedly cleaves

our old-home valley's
thickening darkness then

the breathy *hark*
of a fox-bark stretches

from hunger's or
fear's muzzle

to our
human ears

my brother shines
a quarter-mile

of torch beam and scrapes
pasture & hedgerows with

a tiny patch of day

the beam's dancing
gnat-sparks seem

to soundlessly sing a gauze
of summer night and it's as

       if each
patch

of illuminated foliage is
a grey but gleaming

memory of
daylight's green growth

my brother swings the beam back
& forth through

night's swell

his scraping sweeps reveal
five foxes' gazes as

pairs of pale bright vibrating

planets hanging amongst
grasses & hawthorn leaves

another silvery trickling rabbit squeal

and across the valley (beyond
the brook) these watchful planets

      appear to pull

fox-shapes across the pasture
towards us but

                      no fox comes close

a fox trotting across open ground
in a corner

a fox fast as a granite wall
a fox relaxed as cement
a fox in pursuit

of a picture-edge never
to be caught

dress in a manhole cover under
a fox's stomach

digesting deep space

feel gravity tearing
at your armour

TESS & FOX, SUNDAY 6TH SEPTEMBER 2015

*two weeks before Tess leaves home to start
her five years of studying veterinary science*

the field called
North Pole is

a hill-undulation   a soft
wave of solid

September stubble's
faint lustre

brown-yellow
drill-lines striping

ground with a still

rhythm   ripples left
by crop cut

blue sky behind
bright yet

holding dark as
sun glances

our planet at

September's angle
it seems we

& the hill as
fulcrum feel

light's swing

a season's slipping is
a brief sharp edge

as we walk
stubble brush-clatters

our steps   Tess stops

Tess has found
a perfect

young dead fox

cut out of its
running a red

doggy hieroglyph

brush a fluffy banner
small muddy paws

pointed snout
black-tipped ears

deaf now

what killed this
neat little fox?

Tess asks outloud

she asks me and she asks
her brother   she asks

faded golden ground
she asks the cut

corn-stalks spiking

fox fur then
she recalls

A level biology   she tries
bringing knowledge

she tries
bringing

she tries
she tries

she essays
explanations

for this stiffness
of what was

a supple fox
she turns

over the body   we
clearly see

the simple
blooded patch

of gunshot

Tess knows
that the next

disturbance
other than crows

will be plough
or harrows

tractor pulling
the weight of

metal across ground
to change

stubble to seed-bed

she does not want
this body to be

driven over and

dragged apart

Tess gently grips
a hind-paw and

slowly pulls
this odd form

of gone fox
up from the stubble

she walks away
from us dangling

the fox its

        head lolling

her arm out
stretched so as not

to scrape
the fox's face

along the ground

Tess's long hair
down her back is

the colour of
September stubble

in front of her
the dark green

hedge-line &
a large ashtree

and behind this
the sci-fi white of

my dad's neighbour's
wind-turbine slowly

rotating its blades

through blue

i saw a
hollowed fox as

holl

owed as a
wall of dry

balanced stones

wind held

fox's red

to

gether
　as fox

　　balanced

　　along a gently
　　rattling

　　boundary now

　　i hear fox
　　paws dab

　　softly old
　　hand-placed

　　stones

FOR ZEN FOX

```
flame-fur
red still
                frost
as ice          fox
-threa
                lies
ded ground
halo-ed         cut

with cri
sp mist     out of war
            mth a temp
solid
            late i
young
            peel
tongue glued
into win    off from cry
            stalled grass a
ter's mouth
nee         me

dle-new     morial
teeth iv    of move

ory icicles ment a
saliva fr
            fox out
ost's var   line waits
nish gl
            to be
istens
hung        killed by th

er          aw
```

a fox
each
a fox

a fox
a fox

that's
whilst
a twig

push
a fox's
dress a

warmth

fog hole molecules
rock twig pavement

pavement eternity
into pelt

keep nowhere

UN ENCOUNTER, BY THE RIVER WREAKE

Leicestershire, February 13th 2017

beside a sliding
swollen Wreake

under dangling leaf
less strands

beneath the lantern
forms of

the hugest weep

ing willows i've ever
been

near

you suddenly

stop

        me in   my
        tracks with
        your voice

alert

me to a fox

just steps ahead
of us heading

straight

for us i freeze feel

you freeze also as

unbelievably really
unbelievably

fox

keeps trotting on

as if we are wisps
unseen and yes

now

fox actually passes

within two foot
steps of

us

                        ofthemof
                          youofme
                        ofwhoof

                        anynoone

and just

carries on
past carries

on a way

so i turn hey
fox what

you

doing ignoring

us like

this ? this

fox

now

just

turns

back briefly

stares
as if at

some

thing
now

now

shrugs

now

's

gone

a fox in a fox
a fox a fox of

to dress
a fox's digesting

feel at ground

wall cement pursuit
never caught

under stomach space
tearing armour

is fox night
way sly

a like move
on see

fox night move
like a way

sly
is

a move like
night see a

night on a
fox move

sly way

FOX GO   INGS

I

late afternoon jud
dering along rag

ged farm track pot

hole splashes wind
screen spat

tered with drops sun
light dissol

ved falling

in a hawthorn
tunnel drop

lets ting
ling

light a huge p
uddle wing

ing up from
wheels a fox

flies from h
edge a wet

red fire of brush

shot

across our bows black
socks spla

shing then in

to green to be go

ne

II

night carri
ageway at

60 sud
denly the cent

ral reser
vation's Arm

co yields a

pairoflit
foxes f

ast acr
oss the cat's

eyes snout
-to-b

rush just

in front of
us a double

-act of dog
gish catti

ness two

beautiful o
range rags b

lown through
dark we over

flow with gul

ps of laugh
ter did we

see that we did we saw

it we s
aw them a

do

uble-fox sli
pped across dang

er's corridor then

gone just

us left dri

ving on thr

ough d

(h)ark

ACROSS THE GROUND

by Louis Goodwin, September 2015

turbine's white limbs lash
ash tree
repeated blow after blow
metal on wood

yet the tree does not fall nor strain

perspective
because of course one
is behind the other and

the old tree is not really in battle

but this is only taught
for all my vision tells me is
a story of conflict

half my gaze
sky
the other half
harvested field

connected with only the
locking of branches and
swirling white blades
she approaches

my sister
heads towards the struggle

as she walks into
the distance, I feel
the sting
in her tricep as my own

her hand grasps paws
her arm locked on
an angle
so as to not
pull the dead beast's face
across the ground
whiskers tangling the mudded
stubble

where I would have
dragged
she carries

& Fox feels
the air
one last time
the breeze washes him

where I
would have ignored
she attends
not out of
compassion
for there is no suffering
anymore but

out of respect
she helps the beast to
finish his journey

there is no place for him here
when the plough comes
and so she strains
to help

perhaps
the bullet made him heavier
than natural

yet she persists with
the weight of unfairness
because the feeling runs
deep within her
far deeper
than the furrows of the fields
in which we
stand

and now
fox lays at the foot
of the old ash
the turbine still
trying to cause pain

Fox looks on
amused at the futile
attempt

my sister
turns and begins
the walk towards us
unharmed, unhurt
healed

a fox seeing forever's fog
each fox eye a solid hole

a fox ear filling with molecules
a fox alert as rock

a fox sniffing a twig
that's on *this* pavement

whilst a fox is on *that* pavement

a twig just across eternity

push your fingers into
a fox's plush cold pelt

dress in a fur to keep
a warmth clinging nowhere

smart-fur   red
fox but

a slight

limp   his
left

back bl
ack paw sore

a high

tension wire gently
siz

zles over

head   he
cocks

his leg

marks

a pile of
build

ers' rubble

.

i st
and ab
so

lutely still stare
at

the fox stood on

top

of the ru
bble p

ile he

's ju
st pi

ssed on

fox st
ares st

raight
back

ACKNOWLEDGMENTS

I am grateful to the editors of the following, who have published poems (or versions of) from this cycle:

A Restricted View From Under The Hedge

BBC Wildlife Magazine

Great Works

The Poetry Village

Shearsman

Tears in the Fence

i saw a was inspired by a set of photos tweeted by David Borthwick

Ingram Content Group UK Ltd.
Milton Keynes UK
UKHW011837270423
420877UK00004B/373

9 781913 499051